CONVERGE
Bible Studies

WHO YOU ARE IN CHRIST

CONVERGE
Bible Studies

WHO YOU ARE IN CHRIST

SHANE RAYNOR

Abingdon Press

Nashville

WHO YOU ARE IN CHRIST
CONVERGE BIBLE STUDIES

By Shane Raynor

Library of Congress Cataloging-in-Publication Data has been requested.

ISBN: 978-1-4267-7153-8

Series Editor: Shane Raynor

13 14 15 16 17 18 19 20 21 22—10 9 8 7 6 5 4 3 2 1

Manufactured in the United States of America

CONTENTS

ABOUT THE SERIES

Converge is a series of topical Bible studies based on the Common English Bible translation. Each title in the *Converge* series consists of four studies based around a common topic or theme. *Converge* brings together a unique group of writers from different backgrounds, traditions, and age groups.

HOW TO USE THESE STUDIES

Converge Bible studies can be used by small groups, classes, or individuals. Each study uses a simple format. For the convenience of the reader, the primary Scripture passages are included. In Insight and Ideas, the author of the study guide explores each Scripture passage, going deeper into the text and helping readers understand how the Scripture connects with the theme of the study. Questions are designed to encourage both personal reflection and group conversation. Some questions may not have simple answers. That's part of what makes studying the Bible so exciting.

Although Bible passages are included with each session, study participants may find it useful to have personal Bibles on hand for referencing other Scriptures. Converge studies are designed for use with the Common English Bible; but they work well with any modern, reliable translation.

ONLINE EXTRAS

Converge studies are available in both print and digital formats. Each title in the series has additional components that are available online, including companion articles, blog posts, extra questions, sermon ideas, and podcasts.

To access the companion materials, visit

http://www.MinistryMatters.com/Converge

Thanks for using *Converge*!

INTRODUCTION

When I was a kid, it was virtually impossible to watch television during after-school hours without encountering reruns of the corny 1970's sitcom *The Brady Bunch*. Keep in mind that this was before the days of 500-channel cable and satellite services. In fact, *basic* cable was still new—too new for it to be considered a necessity in our house—so we were stuck with only three TV stations. And as a latchkey kid growing up in the early 1980s, I felt like I was raised in part by the Brady family, the Evans family, and the Cunningham family.

One episode of *The Brady Bunch* deals with middle son Peter's identity crisis. At a party, someone tells him that he's dull and he has no personality. He then tries everything he can think of to get one, including imitating his favorite celebrities and telling dumb jokes.

It all falls flat, of course; and by the end of the episode, Peter figures out (with the help of a pretty girl) that he can't simply imitate someone else's personality; he has to develop his own.

Laugh if you want, but shows like *The Brady Bunch* were a moral anchor for millions of kids growing up in the 1970s and 1980s. Wholesome sitcoms and *ABC Afterschool Specials* contributed to a sense of stability, especially for those of us who were being raised by single, working parents.

Peter was probably about 12 or 13 years old in that episode; and a few years later, when I was the same age, I could certainly relate to what he experienced. Some days in seventh grade, I felt like a misfit and I thought that the world was blowing up around me. Like Peter Brady, I did silly things to try to impress my friends. And like Peter, I made the mistake of letting too many people get inside my head. But it took me much longer than an episode (or even a season!) to figure out who I was. (Some days I'm still not sure.)

After I got to high school, we met another TV middle school kid trying to figure out who he was. On *The Wonder Years,* Kevin Arnold spent six seasons navigating the uncertainty of adolescence during the late 1960s and early 1970s. (The show was set 20 years earlier than its original network run.) *The Wonder Years* wasn't a sitcom; it was a comedy-drama. And through the voice-over narration of the adult Kevin, the show did an amazing job of capturing the feeling of early teen angst that most of us probably experienced at times. What made *The Wonder Years* so good, in my opinion, was its realism and its willingness to end episodes on a down note. In Kevin Arnold, we finally had a character who was

10

almost as clueless about who he was at the end of each week as he was at the beginning—just like the rest of us.

The Bible shows us a brief glimpse into Jesus' "middle school years," in Luke 2. We're not given much information; but in the account of his visit with his family to the temple during Passover, we do get the sense that Jesus is developing a solid understanding of his identity. After Mary and Joseph leave Jesus behind in Jerusalem, they finally find him three days later in the temple, asking questions of the teachers who are there.

Mary says to him, "'Child, why have you treated us like this? Listen! Your father and I have been worried. We've been looking for you!'"

Jesus replies, "'Why were you looking for me? Didn't you know that it was necessary for me to be in my Father's house?'"

Luke then adds, "But they didn't understand what he said to them" (Luke 2:48-50).

Mary and Joseph weren't the only ones who didn't completely get Jesus. People today are still trying to understand all of what he said, especially when he was speaking about who he was.

This book is a study about who we are as Christians. But we can't really answer that question without first developing a basic understanding of who *Jesus* is. If we claim the name of Christ, then how we relate to God, other Christians, the world, and even ourselves depends upon who Jesus is and how our relationship to him affects our own identity.

Admittedly, this topic is too deep to cover comprehensively in four sessions; and I suspect that a thorough treatment of it might produce a volume rivaling the length of Tolstoy's *War and Peace*. But since I have only these 64 pages, I'm going to settle for simply starting some conversations and raising a few questions.

As you work through these sessions, I encourage you to find a Bible with good cross references (I recommend the Common English Reference Bible) or an online resource with something similar. One of the best ways to interpret Scripture is to use Scripture itself, and a reference Bible is an awesome tool designed to help you do that.

It's my conviction that many of the problems we face in the Christian life could be remedied by gaining a better understanding of who we are in our relationship with God through Jesus Christ. It's my prayer that this study make a small contribution toward that goal.

1

GOD'S CHILD
WHO YOU ARE IN THE HEAVENLY REALM

SCRIPTURE
EPHESIANS 2:1-22

[1]At one time, you were like a dead person because of the things you did wrong and your offenses against God. [2]You used to act like most people in our world do. You followed the rule of a destructive spiritual power. This is the spirit of disobedience to God's will that is now at work in persons whose lives are characterized by disobedience. [3]At one time you were like those persons. All of you used to do whatever felt good and whatever you thought you wanted so that you were children headed for punishment just like everyone else.

[4-5]However, God is rich in mercy. He brought us to life with Christ while we were dead as a result of those things that we did wrong. He did this because of the great love that he has for us. You are saved by God's grace! [6]And God raised us up and seated us in the

heavens with Christ Jesus. [7]God did this to show future generations the greatness of his grace by the goodness that God has shown us in Christ Jesus.

[8]You are saved by God's grace because of your faith. This salvation is God's gift. It's not something you possessed. [9]It's not something you did that you can be proud of. [10]Instead, we are God's accomplishment, created in Christ Jesus to do good things. God planned for these good things to be the way that we live our lives.

[11]So remember that once you were Gentiles by physical descent, who were called "uncircumcised" by Jews who are physically circumcised. [12]At that time you were without Christ. You were aliens rather than citizens of Israel, and strangers to the covenants of God's promise. In this world you had no hope and no God. [13]But now, thanks to Christ Jesus, you who once were so far away have been brought near by the blood of Christ.

[14]Christ is our peace. He made both Jews and Gentiles into one group. With his body, he broke down the barrier of hatred that divided us. [15]He canceled the detailed rules of the Law so that he could create one new person out of the two groups, making peace. [16]He reconciled them both as one body to God by the cross, which ended the hostility to God.

[17]When he came, he announced the good news of peace to you who were far away from God and to those who were near. [18]We both have access to the Father through Christ by the one Spirit.

14

[19]So now you are no longer strangers and aliens. Rather, you are fellow citizens with God's people, and you belong to God's household. [20]As God's household, you are built on the foundation of the apostles and prophets with Christ Jesus himself as the cornerstone. [21]The whole building is joined together in him, and it grows up into a temple that is dedicated to the Lord. [22]Christ is building you into a place where God lives through the Spirit.

INSIGHT AND IDEAS

When we come to faith in Jesus Christ, it's a life-changing event. And I'm not talking just a one-time change but a continual change. Please don't misunderstand this point: The initial transformation that takes place in us is significant (although not always easily discernible), but it goes deeper than that. It seems that this God we're getting to know is both loving and disruptive, and it's practically impossible to experience God without being changed.

Any study of our identity as Christians should start with who we are in God's eyes, because how we relate to everyone and everything else is affected by the quality of our relationship with the Creator.

SPIRITUALLY DEAD

In Ephesians 2, Paul doesn't pull punches when he describes what our condition is before we know Christ: "At one time you were like a dead person because of the things you did

WHO YOU ARE IN CHRIST

wrong and your offenses against God." Before we come to Christ, we may be physically alive; but Scripture indicates that because of our sins, we're spiritually dead to God.

At first glance, this seems kind of harsh, doesn't it? It reminds me of the episode of the popular TV show *The Big Bang Theory* in which Leonard decides to date a woman who has recently dumped his friend Howard. When Howard finds out, he gets upset and declares to Leonard, "You are dead to me!"

In a sitcom, this is funny. But if you've ever heard these words from a friend in real life, you know that it's anything *but* funny.

Howard decides that he isn't speaking to Leonard anymore; and the ever-analytical Sheldon (Leonard's roommate) explains it to Leonard this way: "Howard is employing a schoolyard paradigm in which you are, for all intents and purposes, deceased. He intends to act on this by not speaking to you, feigning an inability to hear you when you speak, and otherwise refusing to acknowledge your existence."

As the show progresses, Leonard and Howard eventually reconcile, but not before Leonard and the woman they're fighting over make things right by setting Howard up on a date with one of her friends. You see, in Sitcom Land, hardly anything goes wrong between friends that can't be fixed in 22 minutes. Real life offers no such guarantee.

However, unlike a relationship between flawed sitcom characters, if God tells us we're dead, we can rest assured that it's no schoolyard paradigm being employed; it's serious business.

Before we come to a place of faith, most of us realize that, somewhere along the way, something went wrong in our relationships with God and one another. The problem of sin, although not a comfortable topic for discussion for most of us, is a real one. And the Bible doesn't sugarcoat it: "You used to act like most people in our world do. You followed the rule of a destructive spiritual power. This is the spirit of disobedience to God's will that is now at work in persons whose lives are characterized by disobedience" (Ephesians 2:2).

No doubt, Scripture paints a pretty depressing picture about the hold sin has on us. The good news is that there is more to the story. Paul tells us that God "brought us to life with Christ while we were dead as a result of those things we did wrong" (Ephesians 2:4).

Did you catch that? We're not dead anymore. Not only are we spiritually alive, we're alive to God. But what brings this on? How do we get from the point of doing whatever feels good and doing whatever we think we want to do to "being God's accomplishment, created in Christ Jesus to do good things"? Paul says that it's because of God's grace and mercy.

GRACE AND MERCY

The famous eighteenth-century founder of Methodism, John Wesley, called the work of God that happens in us before our conversion *prevenient grace*. With the exception of theological eggheads and church history nerds, most of us don't run around using the word *prevenient* these days; so I like to think of this concept as *preemptive grace*. God intervenes in our wayward lives and works in ways we probably don't even know about or understand, all to pull us out of sin and bring us into a right relationship together. We obviously have to respond to God with our own free will, but make no mistake, it's God who makes the first move.

The Bible says that before we believe in Christ, we have "no hope and no God" (Ephesians 2:12). Paul says in Colossians 1:21 that we are "alienated from God" and "enemies with him in our minds." These are tough words, but take note that we're the ones who perpetuate the enmity with God—not the other way around. Paul writes in Ephesians 2:4-5 that "God is rich in mercy" and that God brings us to life "because of the great love that he has for us."

I grew up going to church, and I don't remember a time that I didn't believe in God and pray. But my faith really didn't become my own until I was 14. One summer day, I went with my neighbor's family to a Christian bookstore, where I bought a Christian comic book.

After reading it, the gospel made sense to me in a way that it never had before. I had heard the message of Christ probably hundreds of times, but it was like all of the pieces of the puzzle came together for me when I read this comic book. I received Christ that day for myself; but looking back, I can see many of the places God was working in my life before I finally understood what was happening. That's prevenient grace.

GOD'S HOUSEHOLD

This is where it gets exciting. Because of Jesus, we go from being hostile toward God to being part of God's family. We're not merely in a truce with God, or even just at peace with God. We now "belong to God's household" (Ephesians 2:19). "Thanks to Christ Jesus, you who once were so far away have been brought near by the blood of Christ" (Ephesians 2:13). We now have access to God, and access is a powerful thing.

I realized how powerful access can be a few years ago when our church's senior pastor received a phone call from one of his children while he was leading a Bible study. He excused himself and took the call, which was a little awkward because he was the one teaching the study. He later told us that he had a personal rule to always take calls from his family, no matter what. Even when he set his ringer to silent, his family's ringtones were set to override that so he'd get the calls.

Over the years, our pastor has stopped a few board meetings, classes—even counseling sessions—to take calls from his wife and children. I believe that he would go as far as stopping a Sunday sermon to take a family phone call. That's the power of access, and it's just a picture of the access we have with God when we're in Christ.

OUR RELATIONSHIP WITH GOD AND OUR AUTHORITY OVER EVIL

You may have heard the saying, "The enemy of my enemy is my friend." Well in the battle between good and evil, consider this corollary: "The friend of my enemy is also my enemy." When we're in Christ, his biggest enemy becomes our biggest enemy. You probably already know who that enemy is.

"God's Son appeared for this purpose: to destroy the works of the devil" (1 John 3:8).

It's true that our relationship with God changes when we come to faith in Christ; but this also means that, by extension, our relationships with evil spiritual forces change too. In his classic Christian living handbook *The Fight,* psychiatrist John White writes, "You have also established a new relationship with the powers of darkness. Whatever you were before you became a Christian . . . you are now the sworn foe of the legions of hell."

But this shouldn't keep us awake at nights, because Ephesians 2:6 reminds us that God has "raised us up and seated us in the heavens with Christ Jesus." The imagery of Jesus seated in the heavens is referring to his position of authority; so since we're seated with Christ, we also have an enormous amount of authority over the forces of evil.

Several years ago, some friends and I were on our way to visit another church's Saturday evening service; and we stopped at a Chinese restaurant for dinner. While we were eating, I noticed that the restaurant was freezing. I even began to shiver. No one else in our group seemed to be experiencing this, so I realized that I was probably dealing with some kind of illness.

By the time we arrived at the church, I was experiencing chills; and when I entered the building, it suddenly seemed as if all hell were breaking loose inside my body. I struggled for a few minutes and finally had to leave the service and go outside to warm up. (This was late September in Austin, Texas, so it was still really hot.) I was miserable and couldn't wait to get home so that I could go to bed. I knew that there was a probably a logical physical explanation for my flu-like symptoms, but I had a weird feeling that something spiritual was going on too.

I finally made it home and immediately crashed, but I was so miserable that I couldn't get to sleep right away. I felt a prompting to pray, so I did; and the more I prayed, the more I sensed an ominous cloud hanging over me. I prayed that way for what seemed like hours, falling in and out of sleep; but the whole time, I felt that cloud right over my head. It was like an evil force that seemed to be closing in on me. But as I prayed, it stayed back.

If this sounds crazy to you, imagine what it felt like to me. I wondered if perhaps I was delirious from a fever, but I was too weak to get out of bed to check my temperature. So I kept praying. Finally, at some point late in the night, I felt the cloud lift and was able to get some sleep. I don't know exactly what had happened, but it seemed supernatural somehow. I knew that it was all right to stop praying, at least for the night.

The next day, I felt a little better. I didn't have chills anymore, but I could hardly walk because of an odd pain in my left leg. Still, I went to church as usual then spent the rest of the day relaxing at home. But I didn't feel the need to pray like I had prayed the night before, because the tension I'd felt then wasn't there anymore. Somehow I was confident that everything was going to be OK.

Monday morning, I was scheduled to fly to Nashville on business; but I woke up with a rash that ran most of the length of my left leg. I dropped by my church to ask our parish nurse what the rash might be, and she was insistent that I skip the business trip and go to the doctor instead. After a prayer from my pastor, I took the nurse's advice and headed to the urgent care clinic.

It turns out that I had shingles, which I'm told is unusual for people in their mid-30s (my age at the time). Most people who get shingles are much older, they experience a lot of pain, and their symptoms usually last several weeks. I experienced hardly any pain, and my symptoms were virtually gone by the following weekend. Some people might credit my speedy recovery to a quick diagnosis and antiviral medicines. While those interventions no doubt played a role, I'm convinced that prayer was the biggest factor. Scripture says that Jesus gave his followers authority to heal every sickness (see Matthew 10:1 and Luke 10:9), and I believe that I experienced this authority first hand that weekend.

On a number of occasions before and since, I've had the opportunity to pray with this authority for myself and others; and I've watched seemingly impossible situations change course—in many cases overnight. I'm not suggesting that every difficult situation we face originates from spiritual forces of evil; but it's good to know that when we do have to confront evil, we have the authority to do it.

The enemy recognizes who we are in Christ, and God certainly knows who we are. Sometimes its our own understanding of our identity that falls short. We'll consider that in the next portion of our study.

QUESTIONS

1. How did our offenses against God make us like dead people (Ephesians 2:1)?

2. What is the "destructive spiritual power" in Ephesians 2:2? What does this spiritual power destroy?

3. Why is doing whatever feels good and whatever we think we want not a good thing (Ephesians 2:3)?

4. What does it mean to be saved by grace (Ephesians 2:5, 8)? What is *prevenient grace*?

5. What are the good things God created us to do (Ephesians 2:10)?

6. Why does Paul tell the Ephesians (in verse 12) that they had "no hope and no God" when they were without Christ?

7. Ephesians 2:13 says that those who were far away have been brought near by the blood of Christ. In what ways were we far away from God? How does Christ bring us near?

8. How does Jesus Christ bring peace and break down barriers between people (Ephesians 2:14)? What are practical ways we can do this as members of the body of Christ?

9. What does it mean to have access to God (Ephesians 2:18)? What is significant about who is mentioned in this verse?

10. Why does God compare the people who make up a church to a building (Ephesians 2:21-22)?

2

SELF-IMAGE
UNDERSTANDING WHO YOU ARE

SCRIPTURE
ROMANS 6:1-14

[1]So what are we going to say? Should we continue sinning so grace will multiply? [2]Absolutely not! All of us died to sin. How can we still live in it? [3]Or don't you know that all who were baptized into Christ Jesus were baptized into his death? [4]Therefore, we were buried together with him through baptism into his death, so that just as Christ was raised from the dead through the glory of the Father, we too can walk in newness of life. [5]If we were united together in a death like his, we will also be united together in a resurrection like his. [6]This is what we know: the person that we used to be was crucified with him in order to get rid of the corpse that had been controlled by sin. That way we wouldn't be slaves to sin anymore, [7]because a person who has died has been freed from sin's power. [8]But if we died with Christ, we have faith that we will

also live with him. [9]We know that Christ has been raised from the dead and he will never die again. Death no longer has power over him. [10]He died to sin once and for all with his death, but he lives for God with his life. [11]In the same way, you also should consider yourselves dead to sin but alive for God in Christ Jesus.

[12]So then, don't let sin rule your body, so that you do what it wants. [13]Don't offer parts of your body to sin, to be used as weapons to do wrong. Instead, present yourselves to God as people who have been brought back to life from the dead, and offer all the parts of your body to God to be used as weapons to do right. [14]Sin will have no power over you, because you aren't under Law but under grace.

INSIGHT AND IDEAS

The news was buzzing recently about a rare 1913 Liberty Head nickel on its way to the auction block. Word in the coin collecting community is that this five-cent piece could sell for up to $5 million. But what's really fascinating is the story of the coin's history.

Only five 1913 Liberty Head nickels were ever made, because the famous Buffalo Head nickel was introduced that same year. A rogue mint worker named Samuel Brown allegedly altered a die to create the five nickels; and he kept the coins secret until 1920, when he sold them at a coin collectors convention. The nickels remained together for years before the set was broken up in 1942.

George O. Walton, a North Carolina coin collector, bought one of the nickels during the 1940s for a reported $3,750, and had it with him when he was killed in an automobile accident in 1962. The nickel was found at the crash site and given to Walton's sister, Melva Givens, but only after experts had declared the coin a fake.

Melva put the nickel in a closet, where it stayed for the next thirty years, until 1992. Finally, in 2003, Melva's children decided that they'd take the coin to an exhibit in Baltimore, where the other four Liberty Head nickels were on display. A team of coin experts concluded that it was indeed the long-lost nickel.

The heirs allowed the American Numismatic Museum to display the coin for a decade, in honor of their uncle, before finally deciding to sell it.

I'm not sure how much that nickel would have brought at auction during those years when Melva Givens had it stashed away in the closet, but I suspect that it would have made her a wealthy woman. Unfortunately, because she believed some bad information, she never realized what a treasure she had. Locked away in a closet that valuable, rare coin may as well have been a wooden nickel.

For thirty years, Melva Givens didn't realize that the Liberty Head nickel made her a wealthy woman. And for ten years after her death, her children didn't know that they were wealthy, either. When they finally figured it out, they still waited ten years before they activated that wealth. You see, even if you know that you have a coin that's worth millions of dollars, it's effectively not worth anything until you cash it in.

It's important to understand what we possess and who we are.

DEAD TO SIN, ALIVE IN CHRIST

One reason many of us struggle so much in the Christian life is that we don't really understand our position in Christ or what he accomplished for us through his death and resurrection. Simply put, the way we think affects the way we live. Many of us have developed the habit of defeated thinking, so it's no wonder that we often tend to have low expectations of ourselves when it comes to pursuing holiness and gaining victory over sin.

In Romans 6:2, Paul boldly declares, "All of us died to sin." Then he asks, "How can we still live in it?" This is a rhetorical device, so Paul isn't really asking a question here. He's making a statement. To him, the idea of a Christian living in sin is inexplicable, because we're supposed to be dead to it.

In the fall of 2001, the acclaimed miniseries *Band of Brothers* aired on HBO. Based on a book of the same title by Stephen Ambrose, this ten-part broadcast told the story of a single U.S. Army company during World War II. In one of the most memorable scenes, soldier Albert Blithe is overcome with fear while parachuting into France on D-Day. After being separated from everyone else, he hides in a ditch, terrified.

30

Later, another soldier, Ronald Speirs, asks him whether he knows why he hid in the ditch. Blithe answers, "I was scared."

Speirs tells him, "We're all scared. You hid in that ditch because you think there's still hope. But, Blithe, the only hope you have is to accept the fact that you're already dead. And the sooner you accept that, the sooner you'll be able to function as a soldier is supposed to function."

It's easy to spend so much of our time thinking about sin, wrestling with sin, and trying to avoid sin that we forget that we're really dead to it. This doesn't mean we're not able to sin, but it does mean that sin no longer has sway over us. And until we realize we're dead to sin, we simply can't function as a Christian is supposed to function.

CRUCIFIED WITH CHRIST

Paul writes: "This is what we know: the person that we used to be was crucified with [Christ] in order to get rid of the corpse that had been controlled by sin. That way we wouldn't be slaves to sin anymore, because a person who has died has been freed from sin's power" (Romans 6:6-7).

When we're struggling with besetting sins, let's face it— Bible passages like this one can be exasperating. We read Scripture, and we see the way things are supposed to be; then we look at our lives and see the way things are. But like most obstacles we face, we have to deal with them by using faith. Do you remember what the writer of Hebrews said about faith?

"Faith is the reality of what we hope for, the proof of what we don't see" (Hebrews 11:1).

Faith is simply believing what God has said, before we see it. (It's easy to believe after we see, but that's not faith.) The Bible says that if we're in Christ, we're dead to sin; so even though it doesn't feel like we're dead to sin, we have to live into the reality of being dead to sin until it begins to become apparent to us.

THE POWER OF THE HUMAN MIND

I'm usually wary when I run into one of those secular New Age motivational speakers pushing positive thinking techniques, mostly because all of the positive thinking in the world will do only so much good if it isn't based on truth and grounded in who we are in our relationship with God. But like other adherents to non-Christian belief systems, these gurus sometimes grab hold of basic truths that seem to elude many Christians. One of these truths is the fantastic power of the human mind.

Proverbs 4:23 tells us, "More than anything you guard, protect your mind, for life flows from it." Read that statement again; because if you really take it seriously, it will radically change the trajectory of your life. I love the way the Common English Bible translates this verse. Some previous English translations have used the more familiar phrasing "guard your heart," which, while accurate, has sometimes limited it to the counseling arsenals of youth workers and campus ministers giving advice to Christian students about dating. The Hebrew word translated as "mind" (or "heart") is *leb,* which can be defined as the inner part of a human being—a combination of a person's emotions, intellect, and will. Anything that involves feeling, thinking, or doing takes place in the mind. This word is much bigger than romantic love, which is why I prefer the mind translation over the heart one. The reality is, what we think and feel about ourselves and others affects the things we do. With that in mind, anything we allow into our minds that affects those perceptions deserves our ongoing attention.

For years, I worked in urban youth ministry; and one of the greatest challenges I faced was the proliferation of music with negative messages. Although there were the occasional positive hip-hop songs, by and large, the genre was a cesspool of depravity. Occasionally, I broached the subject with some of the teenagers; but I was usually met with objections such as, "We don't listen to the lyrics anyway. We just like the beat." No way was I buying that; I'd seen too many kids trying to act out what they'd heard. When you're young and the music you're listening to constantly sends you negative messages, it's easy to start believing those messages after a while.

FINDING OUR IDENTITY IN CHRIST, NOT SIN

One of the reasons the church has such a sin problem is that we've told ourselves that sinning is still part of who we are. And if we attempt to pursue holiness and make a conscious effort to eradicate sin from our lives, we're often met with resistance from within the Christian community. Sometimes we're actually admonished and accused of attempting to pursue salvation by works. With the best of intentions, a desire to show humility, and an attempt to avoid being called self-righteous, we call ourselves "sinners," even after conversion. Sadly, in many corners of today's church, sinning is thought to be normative and trying to be holy is considered weird. Flip Wilson famously said, "The Devil made me do it." We don't need the Devil to blame it on, because we can just blame it on the sinful nature. The Bible, however, doesn't let us off the hook that easily.

Paul tells us that we should consider ourselves dead to sin but alive for God in Christ Jesus. "Sin will have no power over you, because you aren't under Law but under grace" (Romans 6:11, 14). How much of our struggle with sin is rooted in an incomplete understanding of who we are in Christ and what happened to us when we became Christians? Pastor and author Kris Vallotton has pointed out that Christians don't need a sinful nature to commit sin, because Adam and Eve weren't born with sinful natures, yet they still sinned. All we need in order to sin are a free will and the ability to believe a lie.

In the 1989 movie *Lean on Me,* Morgan Freeman portrays Joe Clark, a principal who's tasked with turning around a failing inner-city high school that is known for its violence and has become a haven for drug dealers. Principal Clark wastes no time making changes. And soon after his arrival, he tells the head custodian, "Tear down those cages in the cafeteria! If we treat our students like animals, that's exactly how they'll behave!"

How we look at ourselves affects the things we do. Far from dwelling on the negatives of our sinful past, the Bible takes an optimistic view of a future with possibilities for holiness—not only after the return of Christ but in the here and now. We're no longer under the Law; we're under grace. So we can't allow a pursuit of holiness to become a yoke of bondage. But we also mustn't allow ourselves to be fenced in by finding our identity in the sin that Christ came to put away.

It's time to tear down the cages. If we see ourselves as sinners, that's what we're going to act like. And that's probably how we're going to view others in the Christian community, too.

In the next section, we'll take a look at our relationship with those other believers.

QUESTIONS

1. What does Paul mean when he says that we have died to sin (Romans 6:2)? If we're really dead to sin, then why do we still sin?

2. What is the connection between baptism and death (Romans 6:3)?

3. What does it mean to be crucified with Christ (Romans 6:6)?

4. Romans 6:6 says that we were once controlled by sin; it even calls us slaves to sin. What implications does this have for free will?

5. If we're truly slaves to sin, why does God hold us accountable for what we do under its influence (Romans 6:6)?

6. Verse 9 says that death no longer has power over Christ. What does this mean for us?

7. In Romans 6:13, the Bible says that when we sin, our body is used as a weapon to do wrong. What is the significance of the weapon analogy?

8. The same verse says that the parts of our body can also be used as weapons to do right. How can weapons be used in a positive way? What might these weapons be used against?

9. Romans 6:14 says, "Sin will have no power over you." Is this your personal experience with sin? Why, or why not? In what ways can Christians experience the reality of this verse?

10. What does it mean to be under grace, as opposed to being under the Law (Romans 6:14)?

3

ALL IN THE FAMILY
UNDERSTANDING WHO OTHER CHRISTIANS ARE

SCRIPTURE
GALATIANS 3:26-29; ROMANS 8:14-17

GALATIANS 3:26-29

26You are all God's children through faith in Christ Jesus. 27All of you who were baptized into Christ have clothed yourselves with Christ. 28There is neither Jew nor Greek; there is neither slave nor free; nor is there male and female, for you are all one in Christ Jesus. 29Now if you belong to Christ, then indeed you are Abraham's descendants, heirs according to the promise.

ROMANS 8:14-17

14All who are led by God's Spirit are God's sons and daughters. 15You didn't receive a spirit of slavery to lead you back again into fear, but you received a Spirit that shows you are adopted as his children. With this Spirit, we cry, "Abba, Father." 16The same Spirit agrees with our spirit, that we are God's children. [17]But if we are children, we are also heirs. We are God's heirs and fellow heirs with Christ, if we really suffer with him so that we can also be glorified with him.

INSIGHT AND IDEAS

One December during my middle school years, my dad threw a family Christmas party and invited most of our relatives, including the ones with whom he didn't get along. My parents had divorced when I was small, and my relationship with my dad was often stressful, especially during my adolescence. I wasn't looking forward to this gathering at all, because I knew that there would be drinking; and I didn't like the way some of my relatives (especially my dad) behaved when they'd had too much alcohol.

My fears materialized when my dad and my grandfather got into an argument that slowly included more of my relatives and eventually stopped the party. I found the whole thing to be incredibly embarrassing, and I felt like I was the only kid in the world who was part of a dysfunctional family. I was one stressed out 11 year old! I'll never forget the words of wisdom my dad's Aunt Rachel shared with me that night: "Remember this, Shane. You can choose your friends, but you can't choose your relatives."

Now that's an obvious statement; but until then, I'd never really seen it for myself. What my great-aunt told me that night liberated me. I realized that I didn't have to feel guilty or embarrassed anymore for being part of a family that behaved like knuckleheads. (Years later, I discovered that most families have people who do stupid things and sometimes hurt the people they love.)

THE CHURCH IS A FAMILY

The Christian community is a lot like a natural family, except that, in many ways, it's even more intense. We have both the love and the drama that regular families have in the healthy relationships and the dysfunctional ones. Sometimes people are estranged for years from their natural family members. And the same is true for Christians. We have arguments, lock ourselves in our rooms, move out of the house, say hurtful things, manipulate one another—all the things earthly families do. But when the going gets rough, we have one another's backs—or we should, anyway, if we really understand the meaning of family.

You see, Christianity is both an individual religion and a communal one. This is important to understand, because keeping the appropriate balance is crucial for building a healthy faith. We must decide for ourselves to follow Christ; no one else can do that for us. There are times when God relates to us as individuals. In Exodus 33, Moses went into the meeting tent to be alone with God and speak face to face "like two people talking to each other." A cloud column even stood at the entrance to the tent while they met. In the same way, the New Testament tells us that "Jesus would withdraw to deserted places for prayer" (Luke 5:16).

41

We must find private time to develop our own personal relationship with God. It's not optional.

But it doesn't stop there.

In Ephesians 1:5, Paul writes that "God destined us to be his adopted children through Jesus Christ because of his love." But no Christian is an only child; God has adopted a lot of other kids too. They're our brothers and sisters; and like earthly siblings, some of them can be downright annoying on occasion. But sometimes, the Christians who irritate us the most are the ones who have the most to teach us—if we'll let them.

For all of the positive things the Protestant Reformation accomplished, one of the most devastating side effects was how easy it became to start new churches and denominations when conflicts arose. Please don't misunderstand my point— sometimes the most productive result in a ministry when two people or groups reach an impasse is to part ways. Paul and Barnabas demonstrated this in Acts 15:39. But it's so easy nowadays to start a new church (or to leave a church altogether) that we sometimes do it to avoid any tension at all. But conflict can be a positive thing; it doesn't have to be bad. God often speaks through tension.

BEING THE BODY

Romans 8:14 declares that "All who are led by God's Spirit are God's sons and daughters." I know that when I'm reading this verse, I typically think of it as referring to individual Christians. In some ways it is, because we are led by God's Spirit individually. But what about the times when the Holy Spirit insists on leading us as a community and won't give one person all of the pieces of the puzzle? I believe that when we fail to recognize those times, we're missing out. Sometimes God doesn't speak until we get alone and listen in silence. Other times, God won't speak until we're with other believers and someone starts talking. It's all about balance.

I've seen this time and time again in my own life and ministry. On a number of occasions, I've isolated myself from others to seek answers from God when I've gone through times of uncertainty or anxiety. For whatever reason, God doesn't seem to answer me when I call. Then, at what seems like the worst possible moment, a friend dealing with a crisis comes to me, asking for advice. Before I know it, I've snapped out of my funk and I begin to hear God speak, both through my friend and even through my own mouth. I'm not sure why God works this way. Perhaps it's to keep us from becoming too independent or too full of ourselves. I know that when I experience this phenomenon, I usually think of the words of Jesus in Matthew 18:20: "For where two or three are gathered in my name, I'm there with them." It's not that God isn't with us when we're alone. God just shows up on a brand new level when we're acting as the body of Christ.

OUR IDENTITY AS CHRISTIANS

Our identity as Christians should supersede any other identities we have, real or imagined. It doesn't matter whether it's our political party, ethnic group, denomination, social class, national citizenship, sexual preference, gender, personality type, or whatever other ways we like to classify ourselves. Being a Christian overrides them all.

That's why Paul writes, "There is neither Jew nor Greek; there is neither slave nor free; nor is there male and female, for you are all one in Christ Jesus" (Galatians 3:28). Paul isn't saying that these divisions and classifications don't exist; he's saying that there's a bond so strong between Christians that all of these things become secondary—virtually meaningless— by comparison.

Unfortunately, if you were the proverbial little green man who came from Mars to observe Western Christians, you'd probably have a hard time figuring this out. In American culture, at least, it seems that political views trump every- thing else, including faith; and we've reached the point where it's more acceptable to relate to a nonbeliever with the same political ideology than it is to relate to a fellow believer with an opposing one. But things wouldn't be this way if we understood what family really means.

I don't usually get into soap operas, but I will admit to watching the current revival of the 1980's television hit *Dallas*. A scene from a recent episode illustrates my previous point about family loyalty. The show's larger-than-life villain, J.R. Ewing (played by Larry Hagman), pays a visit to nemesis Cliff Barnes's daughter Pamela to warn her about going after the company of J.R.'s brother and nephew in divorce court. He tells her, "If you've got it in your pretty little head to go after Ewing Energies in the divorce, you won't be dealing with Christopher. You'll be dealing with me." Pamela reminds him, "You're not part of that company." J.R. replies, "No, but I'm part of that *family*."

It's too bad some Christians don't get the meaning of family the way J.R. does.

HEIRS ACCORDING TO THE PROMISE

Both the Galatians passage and the Romans passage at the beginning of this session mention the word *heirs*. Paul tells the Galatians, "Now if you belong to Christ, then indeed you are Abraham's descendants, heirs according to the promise" (Galatians 3:29). To the Romans, he writes, "But if we are children, we are also heirs. We are God's heirs and fellow heirs with Christ, if we really suffer with him so that we can also be glorified with him" (8:17).

The English word *heir* can mean several things. It's applied to someone who inherits an estate from someone else, usually after the death and according to the terms of a will. It can also mean someone who is in line to succeed to a hereditary rank, title, or office. A third meaning is one who receives a heritage from a predecessor.

The Greek word translated *heir* in both passages, *kleronomos*, could work with any of these; because according to *Strong's Dictionary*, it has connotations of apportioning, sharing, inheriting, and partitioning. So whether we're talking about inheriting Christ's estate, salvation, mission, or teachings, the point is we share in our inheritance with the entire body of Christ.

In another session, I briefly discussed Ephesians 2:6, which reminds us that "God raised us up and seated us in the heavens with Christ Jesus." As part of the body of Christ, we share in Christ's position of authority. But notice Paul's use of the word *us*. Not you, not me—us. We have been raised up and seated in the heavens with Christ. This type of authority and responsibility isn't designed for solitary Christians; it's meant to function within the context of community.

INHERITING CHRIST'S MISSION

There are at least a couple of Scripture passages that come to mind when I think of what the mission of Jesus Christ is. The first is 1 John 3:8: "God's Son appeared for this purpose: to destroy the works of the devil." The second is in Luke 4:18-19, when Jesus reads from Isaiah 61 in the synagogue:

> *The Spirit of the Lord is upon me,*
> *because the Lord has anointed me.*
> *He has sent me to preach good news to the poor,*
> *to proclaim release to the prisoners*
> *and recovery of sight to the blind,*
> *to liberate the oppressed,*
> *and to proclaim the year of the Lord's favor.*

As the body of Christ, we have inherited this mission of Christ; and a big part of that mission involves going beyond the community of Christians to offer God's message of reconciliation to the whole world. Natural families grow and expand, and so does the family of Christians.

That's where we're headed in the final session.

QUESTIONS

1. How does faith in Christ make us God's children (Galatians 3:26)? What might this mean for those who don't have faith in Christ?

2. What does it mean to be clothed with Christ (Galatians 3:27)?

3. What is the point of Galatians 3:28? What implications does this verse have for divisions that exist between Christians?

4. What is significant about the reference to Abraham's descendants in Galatians 3:29?

5. What does it mean to be led by God's Spirit (Romans 8:14)? How can we know whether we're being led by God's Spirit?

6. What is the connection between slavery and fear in Romans 8:15?

7. Why does Paul call Christians God's adopted children (Romans 8:15)? What does it mean that we're adopted?

8. Why do we need the assurance of the Holy Spirit that we are God's children (Romans 8:16)?

9. Romans 8:17 calls us fellow heirs with Christ. What is it that we're inheriting?

10. What does it mean to suffer with Christ (Romans 8:17)? Why is it important for us to do this?

4

BEYOND THE CHURCH
YOUR RELATIONSHIP WITH THE WORLD

SCRIPTURE
2 CORINTHIANS 5:11-21

[11]So we try to persuade people, since we know what it means to fear the Lord. We are well known by God, and I hope that in your heart we are well known by you as well. [12]We aren't trying to commend ourselves to you again. Instead, we are giving you an opportunity to be proud of us so that you could answer those who take pride in superficial appearance, and not in what is in the heart.

[13]If we are crazy, it's for God's sake. If we are rational, it's for your sake. [14]The love of Christ controls us, because we have concluded this: one died for the sake of all; therefore, all died. [15]He died for the sake of all so that those who are alive should live not for themselves but for the one who died for them and was raised.

[16]So then, from this point on we won't recognize people by human standards. Even though we used to know Christ by human standards, that isn't how we know him now. [17]So then, if anyone is in Christ, that person is part of the new creation. The old things have gone away, and look, new things have arrived!

[18]All of these new things are from God, who reconciled us to himself through Christ and who gave us the ministry of reconciliation. [19]In other words, God was reconciling the world to himself through Christ, by not counting people's sins against them. He has trusted us with this message of reconciliation.

[20]So we are ambassadors who represent Christ. God is negotiating with you through us. We beg you as Christ's representatives, "Be reconciled to God!" [21]God caused the one who didn't know sin to be sin for our sake so that through him we could become the righteousness of God.

INSIGHT AND IDEAS

A few years ago, shortly after I became a youth volunteer at a United Methodist congregation in southeast Austin, Texas, we made a decision to move the main weekly youth ministry activity from Sundays to Wednesdays. We did this for a number of reasons, the primary one being that we thought that we'd be able to better reach teenagers in the community who weren't part of our church. Our church building was within walking distance of the local public high school, so we knew we'd have a better shot at getting kids to come to an after school event, rather than one on Sundays.

After a small amount of resistance from within the congregation, we made the change the first Wednesday of the school year. It was an immediate success, and our format gradually evolved into a basketball ministry that included Bible study and pizza. One student who had been a part of our youth ministry for a while was a freshman at the high school, and he started inviting other students. They, in turn, invited others; and over time, we grew to the point that we almost ran out of room in the church gymnasium.

We heard the occasional criticism that we were using pizza and basketball to get the kids to church, but we didn't let that bother us too much. We figured that Jesus had fed the multitudes, so why shouldn't we? (If only we could've figured out how to multiply the pizza.) Out of that original group of students, several became Christians; and the Wednesday group started to become like a family. Some of the students even started showing up on Sundays for Sunday school and the worship service.

The next year, a whole class of new kids joined the regulars on Wednesday afternoons; and that's when the tension began. The new kids, it seems, didn't respect the pecking order that had been established during the previous year by the "veterans." I vividly remember a conversation I had one Wednesday evening with one of our core guys. He protested that some of the new kids were showing up just to play basketball and eat pizza. "They're not here to hear about

God," he protested. I smiled and replied to him, "Are you saying that last year you walked through those doors the first time just so you could hear about God?" His sheepish grin told me that he understood my point.

HEALTHY FAMILIES GROW

Although the circumstances were quite different, that whole episode reminded me of the story of the prodigal son from Luke 15. And it made me realize something else about healthy families. They don't stay the same forever; they grow.

That day, I realized that in a high school youth ministry, we would lose at least 25 percent of our group each year through attrition alone if we weren't training our students to invite freshmen on Wednesday afternoons. It would have been easy to stay in our comfort zone and keep the group focused inward, but that would have spelled doom for our youth ministry. It would have also robbed newcomers of the chance to hear the gospel and join our community. While the urgent need to reach out is obvious in a ministry with a four-year window, it's not so obvious for the church at large. Churches without healthy outreach plans can go for years with current members and even appear to be healthy. Meanwhile, the median member age rises; and sooner or later the bubble bursts.

A church or ministry that isn't growing is dying. I saw this illustrated one summer a few years ago during one of our infamous Texas droughts. At the time, I was sharing a house with several other guys; and we had a pretty big yard that we were responsible for mowing. With almost no rain, our lawn became brown quickly; so we bought sprinklers to keep the grass from dying. My friend Mark, who disliked mowing the lawn as much as I did, had a bright idea.

"What if," he suggested, "we water the lawn just enough so that it doesn't die but not enough so that it will grow?" I thought that was a great plan, so we decided to experiment. You know what? We never found that magical point of equilibrium. It seems that grass just refuses to stay alive if it isn't growing. Churches are the same way.

THE MINISTRY OF RECONCILIATION

In 2 Corinthians 5:18, Paul says that we are reconciled to God through Christ and that God gave us the ministry of reconciliation. This is a remarkable verse. *Reconcile* means to be restored to friendship with someone or to be brought into agreement with someone or something. So through Jesus Christ, God has restored our relationship. But God continues this awesome ministry, using ordinary human beings—who can be unreliable and inefficient at best. Isn't that mind-blowing?

Paul goes on to tell us why God does this:

"In other words, God was reconciling the world to himself through Christ, by not counting people's sins against them. He has trusted us with this message of reconciliation" (2 Corinthians 5:19).

Did you catch that? God trusts us! The gospel is the greatest message anyone could ever hope to hear. But instead of sending angels to deliver it, he delights in sending us. This simultaneously excites, amazes, humbles, and terrifies me. Helping others be reconciled to God is a privilege, and it's part of who we are in Christ. It's also how our Christian family grows.

But there's even more to this story.

AMBASSADORS WHO REPRESENT CHRIST

Paul continues, "So we are ambassadors who represent Christ. God is negotiating with you through us. We beg you as Christ's representatives, 'Be reconciled to God!'" (2 Corinthians 5:20).

According to Dictionary.com, an *ambassador* is "a diplomatic official of the highest rank sent by one sovereign or state to another as its resident representative," or "to represent [the country] on a temporary mission, as for negotiating a treaty."

As Christians, we're doing both. We are residents of the world, but we represent a greater kingdom—one that's not of this world. And through our message of Christ's cruci-fixion and resurrection, we're helping to negotiate peace between God and those who are (like we were at one time) hostile. It's an awesome responsibility.

In fact, that's really the gist of evangelism. The good news is that we can be reconciled to God through Jesus. "God caused the one who didn't know sin to be sin for our sake so that through him we could become the righteousness of God" (2 Corinthians 5:21). Once we really grab hold of this truth (or more accurately, once it grabs hold of us), evangelism is no longer optional. Although we're part of an increasingly pluralistic society that seems to prefer a "live and let live" approach when it comes to faith, true ambassadors are rarely deterred. We should never be pushy or antagonistic (seriously, what kind of effective diplomat acts like that?), but respectful persistence is certainly appropriate.

Once I was at a McDonald's, had ordered my food, and was in line to get a soft drink at the self-service fountain. I wasn't paying attention to the people around me. I was in the middle of a daydream, when suddenly I felt a prompting from the Holy Spirit. I looked around to see what God might be trying to point out to me and I glanced down to see a cast on the right foot of a teenage boy in front of me. He was walking on crutches. I knew two things immediately, but I'm not sure exactly how I knew. One was that he'd gotten hurt playing basketball. The other was that God wanted me to pray for his foot to be healed. I began to wish that I had gone to Taco Bell instead.

The boy with the cast joined his family at a table and I sat a few feet away and began to frantically negotiate with God.

"OK, God, I know that I've been asking you to give me ministry opportunities; but this isn't exactly what I had in mind. This family is going to think I'm crazy. You've got to give me some kind of confirmation that I'm really supposed to do this."

Right then, the family bowed their heads; and the dad began to pray, thanking God for the food. It's as if God were saying, "OK, they're praying. How easy do I have to make this for you?"

So I quickly ate my burger and worked up the courage to approach the table. I told them my name and asked the son whether I could pray for his foot. He seemed a little surprised that a stranger would ask to do this in the middle of a fast-food restaurant, but he agreed. The mother and father, however, seemed really excited.

"Before I pray for you," I explained, "may I ask how you hurt your foot?"

"Playing basketball," he answered.

Coincidence? Possibly, but somehow I doubt it.

The whole family joined me as I placed my hands on the cast and prayed for the son. I felt a strong power and presence as we prayed. McDonald's was crowded, but I don't remember the other customers' reactions to our impromptu prayer meeting. Frankly, at this point, I didn't care. God had shown up, and I was flying high. The entire family thanked me; and I left right after I prayed, so I don't know what happened next. I do know that God gave me the privilege of representing Christ that day, and that it felt great.

PRIESTHOOD OF ALL BELIEVERS

Peter writes, "But you are a chosen race, a royal priesthood, a holy nation, a people who are God's own possession. You have become this people so that you may speak of the wonderful acts of the one who called you out of darkness into his amazing light" (1 Peter 2:9).

Whether or not we're ordained, according to the New Testament, we're all ambassadors and priests. As believers, we all have the privilege of being God's representatives to the rest of the world. God didn't intend for just clergy to be involved in ministry to others—it's something we all get to share.

A few years ago, I gave a Bible to one of the high school students in our church's youth ministry; and I suggested that he read the Gospel of Mark first. This Gospel is action packed and moves quickly, so it's an ideal starting point for someone who's new to the Bible. A few days later, I overheard the student telling one of his friends: "You need to read the Gospel of Mark. I'm reading it now. Jesus is going around healing paralyzed people and all kinds of other wild _____." That wasn't the only coarse word he used as he talked about Jesus to his friend that day. He didn't mean it disrespectfully—those are the words he used to talk about everything. He was a relatively new Christian, so no one had told him yet that he was using "inappropriate" language for an evangelist. The funny thing his, his friend didn't seem to notice either.

Those were the moments I lived for in youth ministry, and they're the moments I live for today as a writer. As Christian believers, we share Christ with the world and then we get to watch the message of the gospel spread through other people. John Wesley famously said, "I look upon all the world as my parish." What he said is true for all Christians. It's in our DNA, and it's part of who we are in Christ.

QUESTIONS

1. What does Paul mean in 2 Corinthians 5:11 by the fear of the Lord? Why does this fear encourage him to persuade others?

2. What does verse 13 mean?

3. In verse 14, how does one person dying for everyone mean that everyone has died?

4. In verse 16, what does it mean to know Christ by "human standards"? Paul says that's not how we know Christ now. How have things changed?

5. What is the new creation in verse 17? How are we part of that new creation once we're in Christ?

6. What is the "ministry of reconciliation" in verse 18? Why is it important?

7. Why does God trust us with the message of reconciliation (2 Corinthians 5:19)?

8. Why do we need to be reconciled to God? How do we respond to those who don't see a need to be reconciled?

9. Why is it such a big deal that we're called "ambassadors who represent Christ" (verse 20)? What does being an ambassador for Christ entail?

10. What does Paul mean in verse 21 when he says that God caused Christ to "be sin for our sake"? How does this cause us to "become the righteousness of God"?

EPILOGUE

1Therefore, if you were raised with Christ, look for the things that are above where Christ is sitting at God's right side. 2Think about the things above and not things on earth. 3You died, and your life is hidden with Christ in God. 4When Christ, who is your life, is revealed, then you also will be revealed with him in glory.

Colossians 3:1-4

John Wesley, the eighteenth-century founder of the Methodist movement, said that the Christian believer's spiritual life is "hid from the world and laid up with God in Christ—who hath merited, promised, prepared it for us, and gives us the earnest and foretaste of it in our hearts."

No matter where you are in your Christian journey, you can be confident and thankful that who you are is not who you were.

Live into that reality.

CONVERGE

Bible Studies

Don't miss any of the upcoming titles in the **CONVERGE** Bible Studies series:

WOMEN OF THE BIBLE
by James A. Harnish
9781426771545

OUR COMMON SINS
by Dottie Escobedo-Frank
9781426768989

SHARING THE GOSPEL
by Curtis Zackery
9781426771569

KINGDOM BUILDING
by Grace Biskie
9781426771576

And more to come.

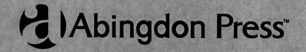
Abingdon Press™

BKM136600003 PACP01354172-01

CPSIA information can be obtained at www.ICGtesting.com
Printed in the USA
BVOW08s2325210813

329110BV00002B/23/P